RIVER LEGS

Kore Press 2013 First Book winner selected by Nikky Finney

RIVER LEGS

poems

JEN McCLANAGHAN

KORE PRESS   TUCSON   2014

standing by women's words since 1993

Kore Press, Inc., Tucson, Arizona USA
www.korepress.org

Design by Sally Geier

We express our gratitude to those who make Kore Press publications possible: The Tucson-Pima ArtsCouncil, The Arizona Commission on the Arts, through appropriations from the Arizona State Legislature and the National Endowment for the Arts.

ISBN-13: 978-1-888553-71-0

Library of Congress Cataloging-in-Publication Data

McClanaghan, Jen.
[Poems. Selections]
River Legs / Jen McClanaghan.
    pages cm
"Winner of the 2013 Kore Press First Book Award."
ISBN-13: 978-1-888553-71-0
ISBN-10: 1-888553-71-5
I. Title.
PS3613.C35726A6 2014
811'.6--dc23
                          2014002428

CONTENTS

for Josh & Henry

and for my father
Joseph McClanaghan
June 13, 1943—July 29, 2005

Better this immersion than to live untouched.

—Lynda Hull

I

MY LIE

We are always moving toward the valley,
and the shadow of the valley
moving toward us. This morning, naked
except for a jaunty paper jacket,
I lied to the gynecologist.
I had read in the newspaper while waiting,
having just told the same lie to the nurse,
of Desmond Tutu prevailing on the world
to bring a war criminal to court,
and The Hague, hesitating, wanting to delay.
I'd read of a girl severed in two,
bent as she drew her bucket of well water,
of lone farmers smote in their fields,
and the slaughtered tribe *Fur*,
a name I affectionately use for my own family.
In Tallahassee I offer up my clean feet,
my painted toes, my lie that I quit smoking.
I study a picture of Bashir,
his closed lips, his cheek inclined
to receive a kiss—
how we share the same cosmology,
the same way of receiving a guest.
I own up to my own crime
against myself which isn't my simple lie
but not letting the world in,
my words swallowed in a private wind,
my thinking too small to deliver me
to the edge of a greater valley,
offering a hand, a sip of water and something of faith
in language, which brings you to me.

INFINITE MELANCHOLY

Lo. Hum. Ho. *It was the winter,*
as Humbert said,

of infinite melancholy. We had mimosas,
and sweaters to unwrap

and return. Detroit,
the big three, a year before we all knew

the money was gone. I spent as much
of the holiday on the bathroom carpet

as I could,
computer and phone pulled inside

like a teenager in a big-brood sitcom
needing her privacy. But

I'm an only child, made sad by
small numbers, me

in my mid-thirties for a few
more weeks, then late and single

which by this age is like hearing,
a mother's sotto voce, *every snowflake*

is different. While you're up,
I'll have another flute-full, but skip

the juice, and let's not take off
the pajamas aunty sent, the warm socks.

Holidays do this, especially
when there aren't more of us

to stop each other from indulging. Like Detroit's car lots
under such blank snow,

which is the only weather
for miles, though not in northern Florida

where I'll return after sweaters
have been exchanged.

I'll take a day at a cold beach with the dog,
which is the right kind of loneliness in winter,

because you're not born to it
like a fox to his fur.

I'll drive by Ho-Hum RV Park
and think of Humbert,

a certain bankruptcy in taking things
so far. For who's to say,

No, honey, no.
It's the same apology I make

on frontage roads, to empty lots
and hotels

so remote they have no one checked in.
No one to touch the towels

and make dirty the sheets for the maids.
Just ribbons of highway

and the many private cars, going
going on their way.

HISTORICAL DISASTERS

I've been in the dining rooms of historical disasters,
(the Titanic and others) when all the good china carpets
    the floor with broken flowers.

I've been on the shoulder of a volcano, forming
my love of lava as its jeweled veil arrests me
    in a museum of ash.

I've also been in the ordinary wrecks and hailstorms.
I've made my list of calamities beyond the news,
    including the time my compass shed

all good sense, pointing to each possible loss
in turn, to washing dishes after your party
    when I ruined it all, confessing, yes

while you paced the driveway, too polite to ring the bell—
I was inside with someone else. It's not like me.
    I make the bed every day.

I baked you a cake, then baked it again when it leaned
too far right. And yet, even as I loved all the way through
    my own complaining, that party

wasn't the first time I felt the world's rough legs
around me, which sounds like
    the most silence,

when all one can do is point to the open door, that frame
of future space, speechless as life is when taken by surprise
    and comes out crying.

PERSONAL AD WITH LOBSTERS

You repaint the walls white because color
is too emotional.
You've committed crimes against the dishes—
roses cracked to single leaves and so scratched,
they reflect you unevenly.
You don't even make the bed.
You prefer the murmuring silk of a sleeping bag.
This is just a start.
The yard's lunar from neglect.
At the grocery store it's one item at a time:
steak knife, lighter fluid, eggs,
as if each old thing requires new integration.
The next day you buy a car with known problems.
You craft a personal ad with the same language:
Low mileage. Runs good. As is.
You add a picture of yourself, smiling from
the driver's side as if to say, all this *and* the car.
Your cry is of the wild, a pelican,
a fish in the mouth of a thin bird.
You drive to the airport for no particular flight:
the arriving, the departing, the waving.
Back outside, the passengers pick up
their old, busy lives,
but your used car is heavy silent.
The moon looks like a sword,
ready to halve our dark planet.
On the ride home you stop at a family restaurant,
lobster-tank calling you from a far wall.
No condolences now, you climb in.
The smell is the bottom of everything.
Antennae quiver silently.
Paragraphs drift from your mouth.
You tell the lobsters you're one of them.
You're a sponge and a lobster
and a ship gone down—a bottom-feeder
marked by the pound.

A HUMAN QUESTION

Summer's accordion breathed life
into the world's little party.

I was there.

You were there too,
a swallow of blue cake, one year dead,

asking, *Wasn't it just my birthday?*

The lanterns, a chain of
paper gowns, bobbed down

and up. The choir grass
and cheap jewelry

of the fence
kept at their unbothered tasks.

We knew something had
passed.

A human
question trawling air

after some thought. After
some right way of doing this.

DEAR TOLEDO,

I lose it in Cynthia's kitchen.

One moment I'm merely a visitor, the next,
her dinner guests learn her daughter's having

a meltdown.

Herman Melville would understand.

He'd kindly take the dishtowel from my hands.
The heavy cream, the coffee poured back in its pot,
and the dessert spoons—to hell with dessert spoons.

In the yellow kitchen he'd read from *Moby Dick*,

...and then, as if his chest had been a mortar,
he burst his hot heart's shell upon it.

That's how it feels, Dear Toledo, but I'm making headway.
Writing to each of you in order—Annapolis, Baltimore,
Cheyenne—

my dad is dead.

It happens in Ohio every day, I know, but this one is mine.
It interrupts even as the guests ready themselves for pie.

WORLD'S LARGEST MILK BOTTLES

In southern Connecticut's claw, a sailboat drifts
from a lesson. The family car,
commandeered by my uncle,
climbs aboard an indigenous tree,
while a rock from our yard blasts
through a neighbor's front tooth:
a first for suburban stones in private space.

There are fires in the closet
and under the bed.
One is set by our dog, Smokey, fed up
with our inattention. Who's to blame?
The neighbors think it's us. So does

the New England arbor club. I say we're elk
a dazzle of muzzle in our prim wood, a flash of our
chandelier antlers when we accelerate,
spinning mulch and gospel music into helixes,
into our bobbins of wild molecular thread.

We're roadside attractions—
1001 lawn ornaments, drive-thru church,
drive-thru tree, world's largest milk bottles—
some cracked, some barely affecting but
a private map: O miniature trail of tears.

O unimpeachable gift shop of the past.

DEAR WORCESTER,

This morning the room is blue. The sheets
   tossed like a bluebird, like one crumpled
wave, stir as I do on invisible strings.

I've a copy of *Dream Songs:*
   all the world like a woolen lover
like a dog who listens with on-again-off-again ears.

My father, somehow thirty-three days dead now...

At his funeral (I held the unfathomable urn)
   my mother bequeathed me a set of blue sheets.
I held them in the salt air traveling off the bay,

a breeze touching at once dune grass,
   beach pea, my pregnant cousin—all of us
home from the cemetery passing into

a fledgling minute—and then another. Seconds of seconds,
   death, a new set of sheets.

ONE RED LOOK

I will admit my love for thin weather and the bird feeder,
  for it attracts cardinals—long betrothed—and common
little finches. Also, it calls to one jay who calls back
  for the lone seed he manages to take.

I will admit my love for the house and corner window
  where birds give constant enjoyment to my withindoors cat.
And my half-love for the ermine stray
  who pilgrimed here this morning with religious stealth.

I will admit things with increasing value, as one admits
  a god, or a god's absence, or one irretrievable confession,
which itself admits whole constellations of light.
  I will then admit the sky into my heart for it is involved in long,

unanswerable war. Here soldiers fall onto young grass
  in their worn coats, as one falls into dream song
and decides to wake no more. I will admit that to die is to never see
  the inside of a kitchen again or a porch-light, embarrassed,

flickering just in time for the kiss that astronauts remember
  in flight, and so do birds all reporting positively:
there is water and there is life. I will admit the strange appearance
  of two armadillos issuing from a row of palms.

They read the following: *We are now out of love.*
  I have many things to ask. Anticipating this they reply,
No questions, please. To each other they speak with one red look
  and turn down a pair of unconnected streets.

I hate these armored creatures who've spoiled my
  love-fest, and who've admitted what I never would say. I will confess
I always tell the truth, while giving nothing away. I will admit
  I spend all day thinking about morning and begin again

after dinner, thinking only of night, while a half-moon spills
  on another soldier. He looks at me, not unkindly, knowing I've left him
for someone else. He who finds my eye from some green periscope,
  who says, *now*, and makes long and final love to the grass.

SPENDING THE DAY IN BED

Already the season has changed around me.
It's summer, so sudden the heat still cranks
through its old vents like a dusty organ I hate

to make quiet. All I want to do is read,
to get into bed the way you can when you've really
come down with something. Lost

under the canopy of quilt and sheet, without guilt
or delay, taking up the passage in *Blood Meridian*,
where an old mule falls from a canyon wall

to the center of the next world. It is without cry
or the goodbye of his species, a pantomimed dance in the arms
of air, freeing him clean of memory.

And my mom's boyfriend at seventy years old
is really in bed and for what we don't know.
He's forgotten the year. He thinks the hospital's

a design studio in California. And though
he's really come down with something,
no one in Detroit can say what it is. He doesn't remember

when my mother tells him things, the nurses
corroborate her story. It's true, they say.
And maybe he believes them and maybe he doesn't.

And maybe this morning is a new place to live. You
in bed and in the desert making sound
for the mule. You in Michigan feeding an old man

for one night a partner in his fevered dream
absolving him of blood-work and bills, anything in the least to keep
from the mercurial edge of the world.

ENTERING THE CEMETERY

The day you died the world woke

to a different world.

A pillow retiring at dawn wasn't
the same by seven thirty. Neither was the boy
in my bed who shares your name, Joe.

How the end of your life was left as a voicemail message.
How in my world you lived another hour while we slept.

The last time I saw you was in a parking lot.

Between small breathing and morning's enormity,
I told you about Joe, then this: *I'll wait for you and we'll
talk about it more*, handing me a hundred dollar bill.

Joe just had surgery

and you were in the hospital everywhere. I saw your thin
gown. Your fingers unhitched a soda from the machine.
I'm certain at one point you checked his blood pressure. Where
did you get the nurse's clothes? How did you know that I was,

at that moment, dreaming of you?

YOUR OWN PRIVATE OIL SPILL

Swimming away from my own
  island, I entered their party
before realizing what I had done.
  Let me begin by saying they were whales.

And we three were in a private ocean
  past the saltboxes and glittering yards.
Past the pea-colored trees and their loping
  boat shadows. Past, finally, the soft nape

of beachfront where evening sounds were settling in.
  I was driven to the dock by the man
I once loved. A few of my things already
  in the car in an airtight tube. There, too,

were my spoiled hopes of living on land.
  You may not understand that I wanted to rest
in the South with one animal who dreams
  of birds and the end of the bed,

but on this, for starters, we did not agree.
  Not to mention adjusting to a new way
of breathing. And what I haven't said
  is that the whales were getting married.

I had interrupted the most delicate words
  of the ceremony but I couldn't swim deeper
or away. And they, startled, kind, invited me
  to take part, which I did,

which is all I ever wanted to do.
  You may not understand also
that after love is your own private oil spill.
  And as a red barge drifts from view,

and the sky becomes another blue
  mammal as placid as the honeymooning
whales, you must adjust yourself, tidally.

MINIATURE PARDONS

Tomorrow there may be tiny eggs
  bought from the farmer: yellow, gray and blue
and his cheese, a small miracle dispatched
          from goats. I may see a llama taking
grass between his teeth, whose chewing into jade saliva
is like old poetry's heartbreak, ancient couplets
  riding the furred neck, a sound at once remote
and inside the skin.

Tomorrow,
  it may be different, the water I was formed in
will be old-fashioned, my family knocked from their seahorses,
          from their dusky corners by my wedding,
a day I'm certain of nothing and all things at once.
My future children layered in mute dust, an idea
  surfacing hotly then hiding again
like the dog's wet tongue.

Yesterday,
  I went to Angola's prison rodeo, and everywhere
a sadness broke through. It shone in the animals' eyes, scared
          and tough and irrelevant. It tired the arms
of the little girl, who raced her horse around a barrel before
losing her hat and falling from her saddle after it, gravity
  a hoof-mooned, dirty wonder.
Ambulances hummed outside the ring,

and beyond that,
  in the dusty lanes, well-behaved prisoners sold
rocking chairs and belts. For five bucks, one took our photo
          in a mock cell with toilet and bed. I posed
with my bridesmaid. In striped shirts
we did our best to look condemned;
  the photographer was so polite, we joked
about a double wedding.

Another inmate held Fat Girl, a black lab
  like my own. And on the way home, a dozen miles
of bayou, we stopped at a bar where a former guard sold
          machine-spun daiquiris. She talked about her boyfriend
somewhere back in Angola. And somewhere else,
I see headlines of priests and sexual trespass, a word
  that finds me as a child studying The Lord's Prayer
for confirmation.

All of yesterday floats up like a pair of hands in supplication,
  or a song broadcasting from Vatican Radio some new hit
and it's me singing for all those children, and it's god
          with a bouquet of baby's breath, sadness put on hold.
Tongues roll back into the mouth's unlocked cell, and I think of
the faithful and the chosen. How tomorrow
  I will be married.

How sometime after, I will think again of Fat Girl learning
  to roll over. I will think of the poor grade
I made in geometry, all the future's difficult math,
          secrets we carry and accrue, the fingers
of my children, fractions of time ever halving
as it does in tri-fold mirrors for which we pay, the grace of
  miniature pardons, of men in flight for a moment
as their horses leave them behind.

II

VIDALIA

On this trip, I'll go through the old albums
  at your mother's house—

the birthday cakes, the names of childhood dogs chained
  outside. I hear how

your older brother picked tobacco or you did,
  and the harvested smell of onions

which names this place. It's Thanksgiving.
  The beauty is ubiquitous and broken,

a lonesomeness of woods and dogs, surrendered barns,
  fields of cotton we could pretend were snow,

and the old stores that slumbered until they closed.
  Your brother still lives here, commuting three hours

to drive a short-haul truck, condemned
  to touch each road laid by the state. Who must wake

and sleep in similar Georgia darks. He who likes old movies,
  which I realize doesn't match my judging of him

while thinking I don't judge. Each thing in my mind something else:
  an image inside an image inside language,

outsourced to imagination, itself a field
  forever filling with snow.

GREATEST SHOW ON EARTH

You spent the morning vacuuming the closet,
its circus of shoes, sweaters fallen from the trapeze.
You spent the morning moving plants in the yard
and bought shampoo, stalling a line
at the pharmacy because of a coupon you couldn't
find. When you finish your minor chores,
mislaying the entire stretch of morning, you sit
in the unfolded beach chair out front. Animals
at your feet and your thoughts going back to
Saturday when the mailman, who spends his lunch hour
parked outside your house, saw the dog and cat moving off
the yard. You drove the neighborhood,
discovering another Lab, not your own, sniffing lawns
like mad. You kept circling, doubling back,
the ringmaster shrugging from behind his sandwich,
the cat come from the woods alone.
Then you think of another Saturday outside,
asking your man: would you say you're in love with me?
Throwing knives at his head, your dog burying
and unburying her ball in the silence.
On your fourth trip round, the mail truck pulls
from your house, the dog at the front door, panting joy
over her disappearance—a canine's most elaborate trick.
This is the easy stuff. You want to be remembered
all your days as your arms around her neck, you two swinging
from a perch, spilling into the sawdust light, and now
for the final act, the one the crowd goes wild for
because of its honesty, without blades, or aerial ballet, you
confessing into her unclouded ear, *love love love.*

EASY FOR A GOD

That's what they said when you, pale
dress, lay your head
on the kitchen table. It was
the attitude of the moth, moments

ago knocking the orbed light—
all life and sizzle
and Icarus when in a flash
of folding he was a shut
and final fan.

Easy for a god.

That's what they said when you couldn't
hack being alone—love again, in those
furtive weeks, married the sky
to your elbow, it happens like this,
in a world made for twos.

That each blue is a waterbed
and your name in the dark
and a liquid
wrench on the whole affair.

It's rain
always at your back when you stop
to listen.

The lepidopterist and a god
let themselves in,
pointing to the moth.
It happens like this,
when only a god can keep out
of the furnace.

After the moth
seized up, you heard

a near church tolling
the hour—a proper dirge
for your ears tuned
to the infinitesimal
and invertebrate. The ordinary.

Easy for a god.

But not for the rest of us. Not you,
a woman in her kitchen caught
by biorhythm's clock,
fumbling the wine cork for a sloppy,
self-pitying loneliness.

Quit waiting for the phone
to ring. Those church bells
are for poets. And that moth
is one tawny ash—
one of millions
to call your future name while falling.

THE WIDOWED BIRD

You hear living on the smallest level:
miniature operas broadcast in grass,
a picnic table scored with years of music:

penknives carving inscrutable initials.
You hear electricity's hum, the human torch-song.

It's in everything forgotten or unthought,
very much alive: wisdom teeth emerging,
an uncle drawing portraits in jail.

There're dream noises too: the name
you call yourself in bed.

The smallest of small:
all the unlaunched spaceships of thought.
All the feathers filling this morning's lawn:

a cardinal clawed and dead.
You hear the wailing among the leaves that is the leaves
and the widowed bird.

Tonight, when I've laid a proper grave,
you'll hear the mosquito revival tent,
you'll hear all talk of God.

DEAR MR. PRESIDENT, DEAR ABRAHAM LINCOLN,

I received your letter as great consolation.

Some days are wheat fields stretching without pause,
till, unexpectedly, gold muzzles a sky so blank
it quiets the business of clouds—

                                               I had four months to prepare.

Our last Saturday, we took pictures on a winter beach.
In one, I'm holding my hair from the wind. Out of politeness,
he removes his wool cap, though he was always cold.

             Sorrow is a crow riding old fields above families
eating leg of lamb dinners, warmed by blazing fires
and blue carpets—their swelling and declining numbers.

Please know how your kindness has touched me, though
it's 1862 & my father doesn't arrive for another eighty-two years,
doesn't die for one hundred and forty-three.

             How words, in a peculiar order, are everything.

Knowing this now is like standing neck-deep in snow,
but oh, how I get carried away! Perhaps you'll have a chance to meet.
If so, tell him to gain some weight. Tell him I say hello.

DEAR DECEMBER,

A day ago he crossed my mind
as I approached my house, each room
a dark woods,

                                a bear holding its breath.

I had no electricity,

no current traveling from the other world
where some slept, some woke out of
their night skin.

I hadn't paid the bill.

Such a small mistake in the off-glow
of an orphaned bulb, hooked, each night,
to a sentimental sky.

O, holiday. O, cheer.

WHERE NO ONE SLEEPS

after reading Jake Adam York's poem "Vigil"

Forget bicycles. The Sunday paper comes by car, closer
to midnight than morning, once
by a man rolling down his window as I arrived home,
imagining he had a violent plan.
He said something almost in another language,
and I could see he was likely a grandfather,
handing me the paper from a pile
as though calming a child's inner weather with a toy,
my lawn suddenly safe enough to sleep on, its growing
in thousands of an inch, its anthills closed as I turned away.
I hated to admit I watch too many crime shows.
I hated to admit my fear of man.
I see his car now and then,
the dog's half-bark over late TV,
his presence, like a light dimmed in a formal room
one barely makes use of. I sat in that room yesterday,
reading a poem about a Southern black boy
delivering papers. He wanted a bike of his own
and in the meantime rode out on the handlebars of his brother's,
where he was shot.
I can't stop thinking of his papers carrying the news of his death,
or his death, which was random
and after reading it was like being at the shore,
but the shore was inside my ears, roaring
as two boys wept with laughter,
then retreated, or ebbed or more rightly back-
pedaled with all sound, with all electricity
to some distant phonograph of sea where no one slept,
where no one still sleeps.

DEAR TEDDIE DARLING,

Yes, my father did pass away, so I'm not surprised
you "had a feeling."

Or that his spirit visited you in San Francisco.

Big spirit.

He comes to me in various ways as a squirrel,
as a dragonfly in the kitchen.

As a foil entering a chink in a fencing jacket:

> His breath-fog squalls my morning coffee. He naps
> in the irrelevant mail, the basin of the sink.
> Letters are written from inside my wrist.

There are hours at which the door to my house is human.

For days he's the water in my car.
Leaky sunroof. Big rain.

He dated you when he divorced Cynthia. Of this
I remember a crack in your car's sunroof. When drunk
he emancipated stars, the incomprehensible glass.

With you he became a Mormon. From there it blurs.
> I was once best friends with your daughter. How strange
> she married a few weeks ago. Congratulations, although
> I hear she didn't invite you.

I sometimes understand. He who is riding with sky,
late with breath, he who is, well, dead—it's a bruise
one discovers blowing wide.

Teddie Darling, as letters rearrange, and the past consumes plains,
water buffalo, birthdays, socks, fathers—I will write to you again
just to write your name.

NOT EVEN THE RAIN

Last night she licked the inside of her leg red.
When I returned home late, she looked up at me
from the bedroom floor, hopelessness breaking
across her face. When I bent for a kiss,
I could see the wet hair pressed in many directions
and the raised wound
running four inches.
We put ointment on it and got into bed.
No licking, I said, and we slept,
the face of love and I.
My boyfriend called, upset by the news,
and I thought of the scarf I knit him for Christmas,
half as long as it ought to be.
He wears it to get the mail.
I thought of that e.e. cummings poem,
the one Michael Caine thinks of,
yelling after Barbara Hershey, *page 112*,
as she climbs into a cab in *Hannah and Her Sisters*.

My students, who are always in love,
can't get enough of this poem.
My boyfriend tells me he ordered the book when he lived in El Paso,
but the box arrived empty.
And I think of a Texas waitress at her kitchen table,
a glass of iced tea just poured,
her dog leaning against her legs for attention.
His tags, a small orchestra, a score
to the heat, her glass perspiring its doll-sized tears
dampening the tablecloth, her fingers around the glass
letting slip a tiny sorrow.
Then rain.

YET ANOTHER WORLD

The wonder of summer: station wagons
stuffed with pilgrims, awaiting vacation's
miracles in the backseat,

of a beach's repeating coolers
with their private food,
the ballad of ice cubes entering a glass,

and the long approaching water,
its sundry mermaids busy
with the rising needlework of waves.

Sandcastles set miniature lives
in motion: from one great hall a pianoforte,
from another, fingers stepping into a glove.

Where a boy renovates
his moat, a woman watches from her canopy bed,
Pull the curtains, she yells,

and the wonder of lovemaking to her lord turns the world
red. The families and the sand make one
giant wave from the parking lot,

and the sea, with its singing that doesn't cease,
climbs the tiny trellis, foam glitters the floor, walls
and their crenellations fall.

There's sweat on the beautiful crèche of sheets,
and tomorrow, there is yet another world:
the wonder of its replications,

its births and pilgrimages, baptisms
and final endings. Its bruising that is sunset,
its tongue in the mouth of rain.

REDNECK VOLVO

It came into the world fifteen years after I did
and already its interior parts are disintegrating—the seat's

widening scar, doors long missing their cargo holds
and the will to stay open.

I've been cautioned to watch its grand leaks,
and Saturday, when smoke drifted from the engine's cave,

I thought at thirty-five, I understand this,
just as I understood on New Year's Eve

when my flat was changed by a guy named Spyder
and another tire blew a mile from his station.

Praise Mike, the mechanic I saw this morning
who works from home, who sprayed his bare feet

in the living room while I waited.
Praise his young son who wanted to

play pool with me and eat potato chips. Later,
when I sat in my car midway up the lift, Mike called up,

This's what a redneck Volvo feels like.
When he drove me home I asked about his

fiancée, and he said, *You mean my future ex-wife?*
It's not understanding something new,

but a new way of moving through the world.
It's like the cashier told me when my tires blew:

Disaster's never too bad because, who knows,
you might just meet your husband in it.

This evening, as my car awaits a gasket,
somewhere near a four-square dinner

and wedding cake, we take out the trash,
we store leftovers, swearing at and swearing our love to

whoever's near enough to listen.

ON RETURNING TO THE WORLD

So different for her, now, to be alone. To have been a dog
among other dogs, a vacation on squirrel-fat hills, the garden
an Eden of bones, free from leash and boredom
and the cat's guerilla war—all this before

her present demotion on our return home. Hers isn't
the human ennui one feels after a family trip, as one descends
to a world seen so clearly from the mountain's altitude,
reluctantly forgiven, and joined again.

None of this seems the case for her, though maybe
I've got something wrong. Is her depression the missing
order of each upright tail now that the pack is gone? The lost routine
of dog whose jaw has loved the throat of another animal.

Unhappy to spend her afternoons brocading my bed with fur,
suggesting room service in a voice I mistook for my own.

DOG MAKING LUNCH

Because I am only
a small part of the pantomime,
the keyboard's secret decoder,
made to make more of things,
I'd rather fall into bed.

Because there's moon in my hair
and the bedroom blinds make
piano music, I sleep late,
saving my promises till
the next day.

Because walking the dog requires
monastic patience, Dr. Snout,
eau de toilette archivist,
jotting her notes: *piss of a poodle, root beer.*

She lolls long enough
for a magpie to land in her sensitive fur,
pecking a displaced hip,
making me see a vulnerability

in her craft,
attacked by a thing with feathers,
she, a sudden and sensitive docent,
making lunch of dead things.

THE LAST FIRE AT THE END OF THE EARTH

It was the summer of grilling.
Even when the afternoons turned
bottle green, threatening to close down,
we persevered at this.

I don't know how kuzdu overcame
the yard. Or when. And how the birdfeeder,
so companionable to paired jays,
emptied itself of seed. The geraniums

are undecided about this place,
though the cactus, with its minor needs, outgrows
its clay pot. The rain comes for the evening,
and the rain refuses to visit.

This sort of thinking, I know, is my
humped animal: milkfed, uncouth,
furred with mercurial gold—human.
It's a sort of optimism and ambivalence

operating at once: in the palms of
scrubbed dishes, the lifecycle of drying
clothes. And there's the grill.
A complexity not of charcoal and

chimney starters, but of standing by,
you and me, half in and half out of
our tragicomedy, our *Traviata*,
though different. This aria is about

the brisket. How you tend to it like a
consumptive thing in bed, how I set
the patio table, locate bug spray and,
as last act, torch the beautiful yard.

III

THE CAIRO LETTERS

1.

The letters hoarded dust, sleeping
  six thousand days—
when they returned to my world,
        from a closet's crowded shelf,
from my half remembered past,
  they came as a story.

Cairo:
  The neighborhood mosque
with its static over the loudspeaker,
        its otherworldly tongue,
calling five times to prayer—everyone drops
  to their knees.

City of music, taxis,
  women selling fruit, incense of
hookah. Our junior semester abroad, studying
        Arabic, Egyptology, Islam,
drinking sweet tea.
  For propriety, we agreed to sleep
in separate rooms,

sharing a bed once in Alexandria
  and for one week at the Red Sea
where a flood washed into our hut,
        taking everything in twos.

Ry stayed to work in a dress shop,
  while I returned to enter
his name in my book of firsts:

First love.

First love letters
        beginning like this:

2.

My hands dip
  into the Nile,
raise foul and yogurt to my lips,
close the mailbox door on the 26th of July Street.

Ry always reading T.E. Lawrence,
  dreaming,
as Lawrence said of good men,
not just at night, but *outside the dust of sleep.*

We saw Hatshepsut's Tomb,
  The Valley of the Kings.
I rode camels:
creatures who fold as if praying.

After I left, he wrote me
  eight-pages daily,
signing his letters *Love. Love. Love.*
I was a sudden queen, crowned

out of the deepest loneliness.
  Letters carried
through Marrakesh, Algiers, Tripoli—infused
with apricot and mint,

a horse crushing olives, fire
  igniting the hearts
of stoves, traveling in their extravagant English,
his tongue a shy tenant in Arabic.

He rubbed his head in my dirty pajamas
  then slept in them, believing,
as Martin Luther said,
that every experience should be baptismal.

T.E. Lawrence said all men dream,
  but not equally.
He was twenty-one: *Dreaming Eye Open.* I turned
nineteen and love was still a kind of sleep.

3.

As I read on, it's like reading the obituary
  of an old friend. From our pension in Zamalek
he moved to the dress shop,
  Shahira Mehrez & Companions, in Dokki,

a nearby Cairo neighborhood.
  When he rang the bell,
he was met by a man with one eye, Rinaldo,
  and taken, by a staircase of thread,

to his new bedroom. Twenty of the letters
  were written from the dress shop,
where Ry ate breakfasts with Rinaldo's wife,
  Shahira, dinner with Rinaldo.

Over tomato soup and rice,
  Rinaldo explained the eye, how driving the desert
under the stars' ancient needlework, he, as one parting
  a curtain passed into his future, through

an army truck parked with its lights off.
  Despite Shahira's steady love in a London hospital,
Rinaldo lost six months of memory.
  He lost his eye and half his face caved in.

When he finally returned to Abi Emama Street,
  he found an old cat bleeding in the road.
He made a bed on his balcony, healing the animal
  with antibiotics from his own wounds.

4.

Ry outlines for me *The Seven Pillars of Wisdom*:
  Lawrence is stationed in Cairo as a British officer.

Lawrence believes in Arab independence. He's one man chasing
  destiny on a camel. I chase after him, searching

for my young self, the girl who receives mail,
  Queen Jen: most ephemeral pharaoh.

I open doors in the desert. I'm riding at night,
  returning, writing, drinking water from a skin.

I'm looking everywhere for Rinaldo's eye.

Ry saw *Play It Again, Sam*, one of our favorites,
  and a woman sat beside him,

I wished I loved her, he wrote, *I wished you were in her place.*
  I read from *Seven Pillars*:

At night we were stained by dew, and shamed into pettiness by
  the innumerable silences of stars. I think of Rinaldo's accident, his

lost eye a crystal ball, a riddle of the sphinx, an ornament
  hung from the rearview mirror in the station wagon of my soul.

I think of the absence of his eye, the hole sewn with gold thread,
  his hieroglyph. I think of it as an envelope, camels kneeling in sand,

calling forth the gods. I call forth the gods, but it's a recording:
  Most of us are only dreaming at night.

The letters got longer. Ry wrote he wanted to come home.
  He wanted to stay:

love, love, love. Alone, drinking sweet tea, he wrote us
  into history. I think of myself as the archeologist,

displacing accrued dust in my campaign
  tent, absorbed in absolute dating.

5.

In letter six he wrote that Shahira
  and Rinaldo were very passionate:
She yelled at everyone in the dress shop,

and he yelled at Ramadan, the butler.
  Over Omar Khayyam wine, Rinaldo,
Eyes Like Buttons, told of being reborn

after his accident. He told Ry, it's the love
  you have with one person that matters,
even in death. He was moved

by Rinaldo, Eye of Thread, who told him,
  it's when you're most unsure of your life
that you're made to realize its ultimate meanings.

Reading through the stacks of envelopes
  what I don't know is that he'll call
seventeen years later while I'm making sense of his words,

If we perfect our relationship,
  he wrote, *we'll reach nirvana.*
What I don't know, until the sound reaches

through the receiver, is that the voice of the future
  is the voice of my Egypt. I say:
                    you won't believe what I found.

In pen, in red hieroglyphs, he made a dynasty of me,
  spending nights above the dress shop
transcribing his romance like a monk.

His vows were the vows of the homesick.
  We were college sweethearts,

destined to grow ordinary and restless,

but his letters outlast us: *Dear Jen,*
   folded into the softest airmail envelopes.

6.

Ry learned primary colors in Arabic from the shop's *galabeya.*
   There's the most beautiful white dress, he said,
      It makes me want to buy it and marry you.

He told me to measure myself in centimeters
   from my ankle to my armpit. Take note of my hips.
      He said: *Measure my mom, too.*

There was nothing Ry didn't write about in those months:
   diarrhea, being overcharged by a taxi, the thrill
      of discovering a mailbox closer

to the dress shop. *What if these letters get lost in there forever?*
   He wonders why my own letters take so long.
      In *Seven Pillars,* Lawrence writes

of Emir Faisal, who worked with the Turks while plotting
   against them, sending secret letters
      to his father in Mecca: *They communicated*

by old retainers of the family, men above suspicion,
who went up and down the Hejaz Railway,
      carrying letters in sword-hilts, in cakes, sewn

between the soles of sandals....

I only remember writing that in Connecticut
      I cooked a chicken for the first time.

I stuffed it with a lemon, and when I served it,
   it was underdone. *Measure yourself.*
      When Rinaldo regained his memory,

he said most of what he learned was rubbish.
  He said what was missing from his education
            was *humility: It's what you give that counts.*

I was working in a donut shop by then,
  carrying his letters home covered in jelly,
            crying the tears of a teenager missing her boyfriend.

7.

He tells her
nothing of those years, choosing to speak instead
exclusively of small things, as would be
the habit of a man and a woman long together
—Louise Glück

Dearest Jen,

1184 BC
I won't keep a journal but write you letters and letters and
letters. I've been gone over seventeen hundred days, just 5,588
more to go! In my dreams I see you tending columns of gold
thread—your loom, a sacred animal. O beautiful hands, I played
"The Water is Wide" on my lute and smelled your dirty nightgown.

1180 BC
I was in the den of the giant, Polyphemus. I seared his eye with a
burning limb. Eye seared shut! It looked like a knot in the olive
tree you love. When dawn rose from her throne of gold I tied
myself to the belly of a ram to pass from his cave. We left the
island and began, once again, our journey to Ithaca—to you.

1179 BC
With heavy heart I traveled to the underworld. I saw Anticlea!
I saw Shahira Mehrez's father & the heroic Ajax who wouldn't
speak a word. I know things about my death, about my way home.
Keep at the lines of your lavender loom. Play it again and again. I
am destined for much heartache but I will die apart from the sea.

1175 BC
What if you don't recognize me, my little buttons-for-eyes? What
if you send Eurycleia to wash my feet as you would a common
traveler? No matter! When I see you, lets speak of small things:
roast chicken, whole lemons, dawn rising from your long thread.

Last night I dreamt your beautiful face was in front of mine.

I love you, my love,
Ry

8.

He checked the 26th of July Street
  mailbox constantly. By his letters I can see

I didn't write as much, By March,
  after three months of mail,

he talked about his plans for the future
  and his flashcards for Arabic.

He always talked about the date,

I get to X another day off my calendar.
 The beauty of time
is that it moves us closer.

The truth: the beauty of time moves us
  many ways.

When he called recently,
  he told me about his wife and son—his life in Boston,

where he'd long forgotten about the letters.
  I thought of this last passage, of Ry

leaning out the window while writing me,

A bubble came floating from the sky,
  and I looked up to see a maid and a child
in a window high above, we waved.

The beauty of time is that it moves on,
  giving us many lives.

In this one, I open doors in the desert,
  I'm writing in return,

measuring myself,
  waving from another future.

IV

MAGICIAN'S ASSISTANT SAWED IN TWO

From the fountain of drool that is dog
and the languor of bathrobes.
From the humility of cereal and fall weather
and the starless refrigerator light
where I stand, hero, god in underwear
From where I ride in the car's worn lap,
passing into one future, then another,
like the magician's assistant sawed in two.
From the pillow which anchors my dreams
like a rope of paper dolls on fire.
From telling my students it was Wittgenstein
or Heidegger or quantum mechanics
that said anything we can imagine is possible, *is.*
From tubs of old soap,
the ankles of my future children,
tented ears of my childhood cat.
From the suburbs of rust, houseplants
that won't die, and my boyfriend who will.
From the great assembly of mushroom and wood,
the metronome of tennis courts, electrocardiograms
and my voice steadied by wine.
From the surprise of fingers touching down,
delivered on a bad day to the lowland of my back,
and the chair pulled closer to mine inevitably,
between mouthfuls of food,
we hurtle through a moment that has only
wind and open windows.
To be remembered for loving avocados
and fog. For loving four legs and not two.
To communicate in the secret language of central air.
To be a woodstove making ash
of yesterday's news.

NIGHT GARDEN OF SLOW BIRDS

The bird was fully dressed, his umber chest, a fire lit
from within dreaming of winter's
  retiring offices:

corsets loosening from flushed roses, frostwater
gone soft, hoses tolling a spring requiem, a mass.
  I bent down to find his ear.

His eyes, closed to me, seeming coquette,
when I revealed myself, calling him,
  William,

with the silver desperation of a spiraling
compass. He gave no answer.
  A dot of blood bloomed

from under his back. The noon sun climbed
a spotless sky, saw this living and dying in my yard,
  again.

I went into the kitchen *for what—*   a dustpan,
And slid him in with wild devotion. Time, a carriage,
  made no sound.

Nor did his unheaving chest. *Did he not recognize me?*
The yard-sounds held their breath. My lips bent to his,
  fed the lantern of his chest.

And again, until his head rolled like a slow match,
I didn't see it at once. Then I saw a torch take me in,
  hovering warmly,

as it did after sex. The cat brought him back
the next day, and I buried him near my car in another
  simple grave,

and knelt without words. That there was just the soft
dreaming of earth, the night garden of slow birds.

SQUARE DANCING

Over barn country, over granite, elm and sweet cream, flying north
where my crib once stood, over

East School where I learned to waltz, the town dump where we brought
our own garbage to save money,

beyond my grandmother's and her mother's granite headstones,
for future grieving: my own mother's plot paid for.

Mountains' glacial cirques and catatonic wildflowers, where bears dig in,
north of the time capsule buried

at day care, my thirty-year-old painting of tulips in the frozen soil.
All this, the Xs

of my childhood, my neighbor Gundela flies over en route to
New Hampshire to a square dancing getaway

with MIT mathematicians. Each boarding a plane in Boston in flannels,
small blossoms of notebook paper in hand,

equations calculated for hexagonal dancing, for dancing in new partnerships
of snowflakes,

where nobody leads, where everybody is equal in algorithms of native wood,
of small feet making roses of geometry.

THE ROSE

Because I had not known a rose until I told my grandmother's story
And then only knew the flower as a degree of our difference,
I am not going to write of its beauty.

And because before I ever learned they could be delivered
in love, and that she sent two bouquets to herself
in winter to make a man jealous,

then bore him three sons before his third heart attack,
before her heart closed from exhaust
in the garage, I go in fear of the flower.

I never knew its thorns, its green throat,
its epic launchings and final acts, its perfume
fresh from the underworld, without her.

I never knew how the rose, ubiquitous in drama
and ovations, stories and special occasions,
would burn all images of itself with its own fire,

as Dido did, her love diminishing under full sail.
Her final silence, the rose. Let it mark me.
Let it arrive with matches.

GOODBYE WORLD

The door opens on the smudged oil
where a stove once stood. Joe shows me
the house on Heartstone that was his parents',
who I assume—judging by the disrepairs
and the yard's garden of rusted metal—
are dead. Standing alone, Joe gone to a bedroom
to let some light in, I wanted to set
and reset the clock, wanted for his parents to fill
a pot with water—an afterlife of pasta
or tea and company. I wanted to shake Joe, a stranger,
or comb his hair and ask what happened, this man
who shares my own dead father's name.
The house doesn't come with a stove
because they get stolen, he explained.
If we weren't so priced out of good neighborhoods,
I might be more understanding.
I might see the weeds as ciphers from the buried,
thin transmissions on the intractability of disaster.
On TV, volunteers on a nearby coast
clean oil from birds with dish soap.
But for each scrubbed back to old feathers,
whole families swim the black hallucination.
Goodbye world. Whole families parting black gold,
gliding elegantly through the soundless machine
that once was a thing called water.

SNOW IN SUMMER

It was iron abandoned from a World's Fair,
or a mirage that for once turned out to be

the real thing: a carnival, set down in a corner lot.
I slowed to look at the hives of miniature lights,

miracle of small hands, and RVs humped
along the back fence

where ticket takers and ride masters,
those who haul this show to each remote acreage,

make their home. Sirens wail.
I hear a child scream. Beyond the carousel

horses leap to their final frieze,
and a young family cools above the fence,

their blue car whirling backwards.
I envy them through my windshield,

as though, with snow-cone's blessing
and a little faith in flecked paint,

happiness can still surprise us.
Like the zebras in the Middle East

who died of starvation, all ribs and rough ground.
The zoo couldn't afford new ones,

so they painted French hair dye on two mules
to look just like the real thing, which they did.

Even here, in a rundown Louisiana town,
at this carnival of small entertainments,

ribbons of tickets part asphalt.
Small rivers in the hands of a family

traveling back in time, splitting
the atoms of air at their shoulders,

pessimism banished until Mathew's beatitude
about the meek comes to mind.

You've won, I'll tell them, passing out
jumbo bears. You believed all along.

THE ANGELA B

River Road goes out from refineries and inscrutable
plants, past the Ag School with its Brahman cows,

who look like old world relatives of bison. At the levee's
highest point the dog smells the bulls from across the road

and sits—the way she does when she wants something—to stare.
Once down here, she who is scared of most things,

tried to round up the cows. Who knows what she thought then,
undomesticated legs taking over, bad hips belonging to another dog,

or what she thinks now, sitting like a nun in contemplation—
a look closer to awe than animal, the very same awe I have for this river,

even with its casinos bobbing unattached, even with its barges
parked on either bank with their dozens of boxcars or coal bins,

my eyesight strains to see. When they rouse from sleep,
and get oriented in the traveling lane, I learn barges are pushed in front,

not pulled as I'd wrongly imagined. And there's the Angela B,
a boat I've made out just once, starting its engines as I walked the dog

early under the angelic span of the 1-10 bridge, a lit halo above
the Mississippi. Angela, a woman who must work somewhere

in this world while living a second life out here,
a young girl churning her skirt of organdy.

MINUTES ARE FIREWORKS

The sweetheart vine hauls itself
along the east-facing window,
and the ant, his unusually long rig,

gloved in the vine's shadow,
traces circles on the window—
an airy meditation on the afterlife.

If heaven isn't a promise to the tiny,
a trading in of small strides and love of crumbs,
offering two hands and a place at the table,

I don't know what is. This is to say that in
our bear-suits, and dramaturgy, our moments of *me*,
we arrive at our personal truths:

such natural disasters come only by surprise,
like the sudden life of a tomato or a rose,
outrageously pink on our annual cake.

Sunset is never merely pretty.
I forget minutes are fireworks and stars
and hours are hammered flint. And so, perhaps, do you.

Time, always dressed in its Sunday best,
demands we attend to it from within
our strange animal skins with our own

hearts, which open on a waltz, a ballerina
in arabesque, on a needle which touches down, a miracle of
music boxes, on the most beautiful-sounding teeth.

MID-CAREER

New Year's Day is a slow train, and not until I walked the dog
  on the levee, did it become itself. I could hear its far-off,
mechanical breathing, the smell of air unburdening itself, fog
  velveting my hair, then lifting to nothing at all. My tongue

feels the mercury moving in the river. I am a part of the unfolding,
  as time moves in a gathering moan. The dog stands watch
over the water, the day, perhaps, not becoming itself at all,
  but a day I remember from yellowed time, fixed and unfixing—

the 70s of station wagons, overdue books with ivy bindings,
  milk bottles. Mariomi Road newly white because I was born
just after an ice storm, another new year, a lake effect in the colonies.
  It's why I have such blizzards, such ice

loosening its corset and giving itself to this moment, nearly forty years later.
  The dog says something in French, *joie*, or maybe just *Jen*,
a dramatic sighing to ask that we move on. This day is for moving on,
  I think, looking to my operatic dog in mid-career, miniature diva

with her big chest and her fear that's in the blood of her breed. *Joie*, I say
  to her retreating back, her scuffed and worn paws, her face,
favoring me with a backward glance. Mercury glinting
  its threat and gift, the boats silvering far below in the Mississippi.

THE SMALLEST BAROMETER

Meanwhile,
I have a forty-year-old's
calves.

I take naps on the sofa,
like so many in my family
before me,

before they
scotch-tape a will
to the medicine cabinet,

shimmering
with talc fingerprints.

What happened
to the barometer
shaped like a farmhouse?

On sunny days,
the farmer's wife came out
for cow milking.

The farmer saddled
storm clouds
as if they were his horse—

his vinegar smile, shaking
one angry fist at God.

AN APOLOGY FOR SOME OF THE WAYS THE WORLD WENT WRONG

You study the portraits of the dead
from last week's paper, tracing a finger over brows,

lapels, over the celestial rise of shoulders.
Their eyes burn like rain, like torchlight
caught in the slow face of a creek.

Newsprint from a woman's hair darkens your finger,
while she stares at you, as they all do,
from an old configuration of the world.

You read their names, understanding
their fate in the imperfect way the living do,

and feel the rain as a Ferris wheel—
toes brushing your cheek
as one page is turned, then another,
until you've gone beyond death,

holding the newspaper to the window
and standing, just so, behind the soldiers,
close enough to smell their buried soap, their sweat.

Close enough to whisper:
I am the creek. I am the sound of dirt breaking into song.

THE GARDEN DISTRICT

Sometimes I like this raft of land, this porch
and low flying swing, this Southern grass grown frizzy,

made elegant for a few hours after mowing
despite the morning dog shit

we hadn't gotten around to yet. Other times, pinwheels
of shame bore in me—my neighbors,

in box-store uniforms, waiting in the heat
for a bus that comes so irregularly,

it's nothing less than an abusive lover.
Other times, boards seem to filter all light

from the neighboring houses, the Lincoln theater
at the right slant of descending sun glows gold,

the barber shop sign's black-inked blow dryer
stenciled out front

like a quaint, loaded gun,
the social club and House of Glamour.

Sometimes I'm outside this hot light. Sometimes,
I drive my black lab to the river in my Volvo,

public radio a minor static below a woman yelling
to me from her front porch, patron saint

of what's beyond us, dividing us: *let that nigger go,*
at which my black lab wags and bumps like crazy,

her tongue licking the air for nonspecific love
contained in each moment of each thought.

STEPPING INTO A FURNACE

I was going home for Christmas, the idea leaving me
like the heat, which mostly didn't work.
I drove miles in uninterrupted dark,
single traveler, broken
by one set of headlights moving past,
illuminating wings in the bed of my truck.
Somehow I was unsurprised,
as though the angel appeared by appointment.
I stopped and he climbed into the cab (his wings so yielding),
fumbling with his seatbelt. The radio
played holiday music, but I heard something
like wind in a box. I drove him
to a small motel: its honky-tonk
of ice machines, its lobby's blank face.
We opened the tiny soaps and the festive
chocolates bought from the front desk.
It would all, as we already knew,
stepping into the furnace, forging our wings
and flying over the Gulf,
form the last or almost last poem.
I felt with one free hand, twin gardens
of stars, an obdurate coast,
the velvet alphabet of pines.

RIVER LEGS

This is for the prayer wheel and carnival barker, oddities
pickled in a jar, for a banjo tuned by reckless angels,
and a museum piece whose placard reads: *Life*.

This is for the maps, for the border with Mexico
and men on fire who fold their clothes in the desert—O sleep,
and for the last dance in the arms of saguaro.

This is for promises met with death,

for a little money to buy a tin roof. For Mexican brides,
mi amor, this line shedding tears for
all the dry eyes, for veils trembling in sun.

This is for the animals—those with fur cut
away, the tuskless and mounted, those in hunting
season closing their eyes to the grass.

For all the eggs laid in miniscule palaces,

for beginnings and for infinity's
exotic locale in the den of human hearts. Forever
is fireworks made from a wand of chalk.

For those who make love and those who steal robes,
for motels holding our stories in their rugs
and uncertain bedding pilled by dreams.

This is for you—a dirge, a carousel tune, the ice
and the wooly mammoth in perfect union—
the unequaled arms of a lover underground.

For tupperware containers
holding the unclaimed dead—for the labels
a coroner made with a pen—for instance,

River Legs. How can I say they are human parts
washed to shore? How can I go on thinking *beautiful* and
poetry. And: *River Legs meets Lone Heart, marries.*

ACKNOWLEDGMENTS

"My Lie," *The New Yorker* & *Best American Poetry 2013*

"Infinite Melancholy," & "Last Fire at the End of the Earth,"
    The Southern Review

"The Smallest Barometer," *Alaska Quarterly Review*

"Goodbye World," & "The Widowed Bird", (published as "What You
    Hear When You Listen to Dying Trees,")*The Pinch*

"Miniature Pardons" (published as "The Beginning"), *Shenandoah* online

"Stepping Into a Furnace," *Hawaii Women's Journal*

"One Red Look," *New England Review*

"On Returning to the World,"."Easy for a God" & "Spending the Day
    in Bed," *Sycamore Review*

"Greatest Show on Earth," *AGNI* online

"World's Largest Milk Bottles" & "Yet Another World" (published
    as "Hidden Industry"), *Hotel Amerika*

"Prosody of a Horse," *Barrow Street*

"An Apology for Some of the Ways the World Went Wrong,"
    Southern Humanities Review

"Historical Disasters," *Spoon River Poetry Review*

"River Legs," *Georgetown Review*

"Magician's Assistant Sawed in Two," *FIELD*

"A Human Question," *Columbia Poetry Review*

"Personal Ad With Lobsters," *Post Road*

"Dear Toledo," *Third Coast*

"Dear Mr. President, Dear Abraham Lincoln," *Cream City Review*

"Your Own Private Oil Spill," *The Missouri Review*'s poem of the week

"Night Garden of Slow Birds," *Cimarron Review*

"Redneck Volvo," & "The Rose," *The Florida Review*

ABOUT THE AUTHOR

Jen McClanaghan's work has appeared in *The New Yorker*, *Best American Poetry 2013*, *The Southern Review*, and *New England Review*. She is an assistant professor and writer in residence at Salve Regina University in Rhode Island, where she lives with her husband and son.

As a community of literary activists devoted to bringing forth a diversity of voices through works that meet the highest artistic standards, Kore Press publishes women's writing to deepen awareness and advance progressive social change.

Kore Press has been publishing the creative genius of women writers since 1993 to foster equitable public discourse and a diverse, accurate, historic record.

* Since its inception in 1923, *Time Magazine* has had one female editor.

* Since 1948, the Pulitzer Prize for Fiction has gone to 42 men and 17 women.

* Only 12 of 109 Nobel Prizes for Literature have gone to women. Three of the 12 female winners were in the last decade.

If you'd like to purchase a Kore Press book or make a tax-deductible contribution to the vital project of publishing contemporary women's literature, go here: **korepress.org.**